SURVIVING GRACE

Trish Vradenburg

BROADWAY PLAY PUBLISHING INC
224 E 62nd St, NY, NY 10065
www.broadwayplaypub.com
info@broadwayplaypub.com

SURVIVING GRACE
© Copyright 2003 by Trish Vradenburg

All rights reserved. This work is fully protected under the copyright laws of the United States of America. No part of this publication may be photocopied, reproduced, stored in a retrieval system, or transmitted, in any form or by any means, electronic, mechanical, recording, or otherwise, without the prior permission of the publisher. Additional copies of this play are available from the publisher.

Written permission is required for live performance of any sort. This includes readings, cuttings, scenes, and excerpts. For all rights please contact Broadway Play Publishing Inc.

First printing: June 2003; this edition: Aug 2017
I S B N: 978-0-88145-217-4

Book design: Marie Donovan
Word processing: Microsoft Word for Windows
Typographic controls: Xerox Ventura Publisher 2.0 P E
Typeface: Palatino
Copy editing: Sue Gilad

ORIGINAL PRODUCTION

SURVIVING GRACE was produced by Nina Benton at the Union Square Theater in New York. The cast and creative contributors were:

KATE GRISWALD	Illeana Douglas
LENNY THE DOORMAN	James Hindman
GRACE GRISWALD	Doris Belack
JACK GRISWALD	Jerry Grayson
MADGE WELLINGTON	Linda Hart
MARTY	James Hindman
VARIOUS DOCTORS	James Hindman
SAM GELMAN	Armand Schultz
LORNA	Cynthia Darlow
MORTON SELIGMAN	James Hindman
NURSE PAM	Linda Hart

Director .... Jack Hofsiss
Set design .... David Gallo
Costume design .... Ann Hould-Ward
Lighting design .... Russell H Champa
Original music & sound design
.... Guy Sherman/Aural Fixation
Casting .... Jay Binder
Musical staging .... Robert La Fosse
Production stage manager .... Joshua Halperin
Production manager .... Kai Brothers
General management
.... Richard Frankel Productions/Jo Porter
Press representative .... Barlow/Hartman

CHARACTERS & SETTING

KATE GRISWALD, 36
GRACE GRISWALD, 65
JACK GRISWALD, 68
SAM GELMAN, 38
LORNA, 52
MADGE WELLINGTON, 50s
various others (played by one person)

Time: The present

Place: New York City; Tenafly, N J; Chicago; Miami

Although the medical possibilities are very real, at present the story on these pages is a fantasy, a wish, an impossible dream. The same words that were said to Galileo, Newton, Edison, Pasteur, Einstein, Curie, Salk, Sabin and whoever dreamed up a fax.

Yesterday's dream is today's reality.

ACT ONE

(The stage is divided into separate playing spaces. Across the back wall are a series of photos. The stage is dark. On the first space there is a black and white photo, circa 1958, of GRACE GRISWALD, *twenty-two. Her eyelashes are penciled in, creating longer lashes, her chin is softened with pencil, her nose is made thinner. Across the second screen is* GRACE, *thirty-six, with* KATE GRISWALD, *seven, circa 1972.* GRACE's *nose has been erased, her waist has been tapered so dramatically by coloring it in with black ink that her arm is merely a peg limb.* KATE's *nose has been shortened and her hair given a drawn-on flip. On the third screen is a picture of* KATE, *circa 1985, in college. Her chin has been diminished with pencil, her eyebrows have been enhanced, her cheeks have some blush.)*

(Lights up on KATE GRISWALD, *mid-thirties, standing outside of her apartment. She talks to the audience.)*

KATE: My mother used to say that if every woman accurately remembered childbirth—or knew about the more prolonged agony of living with a teenaged daughter—no family would have more than one child. People remember what they can live with.

I am a writer—a profession that in its purest state sets you free...free to dream, to wish, to create what could have been. And so, with the humor that makes life tolerable, I offer some truths, some memories, some possibilities....

(Lights up on KATE GRISWALD's *apartment. It is functional, not very neat.* KATE *walks in and picks up her cell phone, her constant appendage. While she talks, she goes over papers. This is a not a woman who is satisfied accomplishing only one thing at a time.)*

KATE: Listen, Marty, I'm not casting Simon Rudolph. He's unlikable. This is not a good trait for a series regular.

(A buzzer rings.)

KATE: Hold on, that's my doorman. *(Pushes the intercom button)* Speak to me, Lenny.

LENNY: *(Thru intercom)* Your mother's on her way up.

KATE: Thanks, Lenny.

LENNY: She told me I didn't look mean enough to scare off looters should they want to storm the building. She made me practice a don't-make-me-kill-you face.

KATE: I know that face. You can take on anyone now. Thanks, Lenny.

LENNY: Yep!

KATE: *(Back on phone)* My mother. She drove in from Jersey.

(The doorbell rings.)

KATE: It's open.

(The doorbell rings again.)

KATE: It's open. Okay, Marty, let's go over the numbers.

*(*GRACE GRISWALD, *sixties,* KATE's *mother enters.* GRACE *is handsomely dressed, with impeccably coiffed gray hair, her trademark pearls, the perfect lady.* KATE *mouths a "hi" to her.)*

GRACE: The door was wide open.

ACT ONE

KATE: Be off in a minute.

GRACE: *(Shakes her head)* I could have been a mass murderer.

KATE: Give me the overnights.

GRACE: There are ten thousand rapes every day on Live At Five.

KATE: Can we talk about this in a minute?

(GRACE goes to check various ways to lock the door.)

KATE: A twenty share in *Cleveland*? The network ought to kiss our ass.

GRACE: Katie! Language! If you're busy, I'll just visit neighbors in the building.

(KATE shakes her head no as GRACE opens the door to leave.)

KATE: No, Marty, you take care of it. Gotta go.

(KATE hangs up phone and comes to kiss her mother.)

KATE: Hi, Mom. Happy birthday. I'm sorry I'll be late tonight for your party.

GRACE: I just wish you could be there.

KATE: I told you I'll be there in time for the toasts.

GRACE: If you can't, you can't.

KATE: But I will.

GRACE: But if you can't, you can't.

KATE: I will!

GRACE: I'll understand. You're a very busy lady. It's wonderful you're so important.

KATE: Believe me, I'm not so important.

GRACE: Then come early to my party.

(The phone rings.)

KATE: Like you said, very important. *(Answers phone)* Kate Griswald. Hi, Dan. How are you?

GRACE: Look at this lampshade... dust catcher.

KATE: The main set's a given, Dan. Five thousand. That's what I have, that's what I pay. Fine. Get back to me. *(Hangs up phone angrily)* Shmuck.

GRACE: Language. Trouble?

KATE: Nothing that won't work itself out. *(Sotto)* Could I use a cigarette.

GRACE: Did you say cigarette?

KATE: Bats don't hear that well.

GRACE: Forty-three thousand fatalities a year from that death weed. I cut out some articles I have with me. *(Takes out some articles. A ticket drops.)*

KATE: What's that? You got a ticket?

GRACE: *(Quickly puts into pocket)* I was going five-miles-an-hour in the fast lane on The G W Bridge. These days they fine you for being cautious.

(The phone rings.)

KATE: *(Exasperated)* It doesn't stop. *(Answers phone)* Kate Griswald. Oh, great, what's Madge's problem this time?

GRACE: *(Reminiscing)* I remember the days I was rushing—another meeting, another fund-raiser, another day of shopping. Funny how we throw time away....

KATE: *(Has heard this before)* But we're not in the THE-A-TUH. No two-month rehearsals. It's T V. Five days, you're out. *(Beat)* Forget massaging her ego. It's time for me to play "bad cop." I'll get there as soon as I can. *(Hangs up)* Damn. *(To GRACE)* Mom, I have to go to the studio. I'm really sorry.

ACT ONE 5

GRACE: It's no big deal. I only crossed state lines. *(Quickly)* I'm kidding.

KATE: No, this is really awful.

GRACE: Stop. You feel worse than I do. Really. I just... *(The words tumble out)* ...miss you. Sorry. I'm trying hard not to give you guilt.

KATE: You converted?

GRACE: I want you to be happy and successful like you are.

KATE: Like those two go hand in hand?

GRACE: You aren't happy? Do you think it's because you're in-between...fellas?

KATE: Mom, I forgot to tell you. I married a prominent plastic surgeon. We have two-point-three gorgeous kids and a poodle named Lickey. They all got into Harvard. Even Lickey.

GRACE: Funny girl.

KATE: I have a "fella." His name's Charlie, remember?

GRACE: Katie, he's married. You're the one who did so well on your S A Ts—see if you can find what doesn't belong.

KATE: He's been divorced a year now. And he is Jewish.

GRACE: Believe it or not there are a couple of Jews I'm not so crazy about. This Charlie of yours is a humorless person with pasty skin—a dominant genetic trait. But it's your life, your decision.

KATE: This is good news.

GRACE: Did I mention Ceal Janowitz has a lovely nephew who's dying to meet you?

KATE: What happened to "my life, my decision"?

GRACE: It wasn't working out. I'm telling you forty more pounds on the liquid diet, Melvin'll be a knockout. I'll set it up. He'd be lucky to get someone as beautiful as you.

KATE: Yeah, that's me—gorgeous.

GRACE: Some more makeup, a chic haircut so the world could see your face, you'd be breathtaking. Like in the picture I showed him. *(She shows the photo to KATE as she takes out a hankie.)*

KATE: Oh, my god. You have to stop touching up my photos. *(Looking at pictures again)* What did you use to get rid of my hair? Whiteout?

GRACE: And pink crayon for blush. See how it lights up your face?

(Off KATE's look)

GRACE: Forget it. I think you're perfect. *(Beat)* So you're keeping your hair brown?

KATE: My friends say my color looks great.

GRACE: You're comparing me to a friend? Everyone has an agenda. Only a mother loves you enough to hurt you. Come here, you have some shmootz on you.

(She puts her hankie to her tongue and then out to wipe KATE's face. KATE pulls away, spills her drink on her sweater. She immediately gets flustered.)

KATE: You know I hate that saliva thing.

GRACE: I'm sorry.

KATE: Now I have to change my sweater.

GRACE: Don't worry, I'll get the stain out with club soda. I hope that works on synthetics.

KATE: It's not synthetic. It's cashmere.

ACT ONE

GRACE: There's a switch. Cashmere made to look synthetic.

KATE: *(Sighs)* You win. I paid extra to get polyester.

(KATE *exits.* GRACE *immediately takes out club soda from her handbag and starts to clean the sweater. She looks at the phone. She thinks for a minute and then dials a number. On the other side of the stage,* JACK GRISWALD, *late sixties, still attractive, answers phone.)*

JACK: Hello.

GRACE: Hello, Jack.

JACK: Where are you?

GRACE: In Katie's apartment.

JACK: I bought cinnamon bagels for you.

GRACE: *(Smiles gently)* All right, Jack, so maybe I won't leave you.

JACK: I was worried. Sometimes you forget where you're going.

GRACE: They're called senior moments.

JACK: You didn't tell Katie what I said?

(KATE *enters, hearing the end of the conversation.)*

GRACE: No. Jack, listen. Why don't we try being a little easier on each other?

JACK: I don't know what happens. It's not that I don't care.

GRACE: I know. Me, too. *(Hangs up. Looks at* KATE*)* Look how much better that looks, darling.

KATE: Another fight with Daddy?

GRACE: Minor skirmish. *(Shrugs)* Retirement's not easy for a big-shot dentist. He needs someone to boss. I was elected.

KATE: You don't have to take it.

GRACE: *(Dryly)* You're right, I have so many alternatives. I was thinking medical school. *(She looks at plaque)* Now *this* is my pride. "Best Achievement in Writing for a Comedy Series." That was some night. Like seeing myself succeed. Not that I have your talent. I'm not saying that. Did I ever tell you I once took a course from the great Morton Seligman?

KATE: *(Has heard this a million times)* Said you were gifted.

GRACE: To the whole class. Grace Griswald has a gift for words. As God is my witness...a gift for words. Mister Seligman— *(A little smitten, remembering)* —a dead ringer for Tyrone Power—a beautiful male specimen...

KATE: I wonder where he is now?

GRACE: Chicago.

KATE: *(Surprised she knows)* Really?

GRACE: *(Shrugs)* I read *People* magazine at the beauty parlor. Anyway, he said he expected to read great things from me one day.

KATE: You could have done both.

GRACE: If I could have, I would have. It was a different world then. I had a family, a husband, volunteer work. I don't regret it. *You* could have it all—including a wonderful family like your sister, Gwen.

KATE: Five kids in five years. Gwen always had trouble with that "no" concept. Mom, I'm more than a vessel to the next generation.

GRACE: It's my birthday. I don't want to fight.

KATE: Like I do.

(KATE's cell phone rings.)

ACT ONE

KATE: *(Snaps back to her business mode)* I'm on my way, Marty. Don't let that bitch slit her wrist until I get there. I want to see the blood. *(Hangs up phone)*

GRACE: Katie, Do you think you should be as...blunt as you are? People respect a lady.

KATE: Mom, eighty percent of T V writers are male. I don't talk like a sailor, the room gets silent.

GRACE: You're right. A woman has to fight for what she gets. That's why you're a success. I'm not saying socially, of course, but businesswise.

KATE: Tell you what, Mom, for a special bonus present you can draw me pregnant in all those pictures and I'll pretend I don't mind.

(They hug each other goodbye.)

GRACE: You make me so proud, darling.

KATE: *(Almost like a little girl)* Do I?

GRACE: *(Touches* KATE's *hair)* Back to blonde... For me...

(Lights up on MADGE WELLINGTON, *fifties, actress in her dressing room.)*

MADGE: *(Lifting script) These lines are crap*!

*(*KATE *walks in, ready to do battle.)*

MADGE: Tennessee Williams was a writer. When I did his plays I was working with an artiste.

KATE: Williams had a little more time and a lot more alcohol. Madge, we cannot shut down production to debate the motivation of every line you say. Your character is a divorced waitress who moves from restaurant to restaurant because she can't hold on to a job. She has two kids, a dead-beat ex-husband and an asthmatic Beagle. Her motivation is survival. Like everyone working on this show. So here's the deal: your behavior has to change. It's costing time, morale and money. This is show *BUSINESS*. And when we do no show, we do no business.

MADGE: Are you threatening me?

KATE: I'm giving you options.

MADGE: Well, it *sounds* like you're threatening me.

KATE: Options can sound that way.

MADGE: How dare you. I can see that you never eat lunch in this town again! I am one of the greats!

KATE: Which is the only reason we're having this discussion. Let me give you some T V reality. Actors are disposable. Writers fail *UP*. Fact of life. But if you stay and "Order Up" is a hit, you—the star—will be lauded, featured on magazine covers, add gold statues to your collection. Best of all, *you will be rich*. In three years, you will be able to demand obscene amounts of money, more creative control, and remove the bitch who stands before you. If you leave, you can play Medea in summer stock with Charles Nelson Reilly.

MADGE: *(Coldly)* I'll discuss these "options" with my advisors.

(MADGE *grabs* MARTY's *cell and walks to other side in a huff.*)

MARTY: *(Dramatically)* Divas. By the by, I personally went to the florist for your mother. I also got you a little gift while I was there. I couldn't resist.

(MARTY *hands* KATE *the gift. She takes out a pillow and reads:)*

KATE: "Mirror, mirror on the wall. I am my mother after all." *(Beat)* That's vicious.

MARTY: Thank you.

KATE: *(A little worried)* You don't really think I am, do you?

ACT ONE

MARTY: Aren't we all?

MADGE: *(To* KATE*)* I discussed it with my agent, my attorney, and my husband. We all agreed that I would honor my commitment and stay... *(Warningly)* For now. *(Exits grandly)*

*(*MARTY *and* KATE *look at cell phone number.)*

MARTY: She made one call.

(They both look at the number.)

KATE/MARTY: *(Of course)* Bergdorf's.

(To dark. Light on GRACE, *cleaning up after party.* KATE *rushes in, still wearing what she had on in the afternoon.)*

KATE: Good party?

JACK: Fine, except your mother forgot my name.

GRACE: Senior moment.

KATE: So I missed the toasts?

GRACE: Only by an hour.

KATE: I'm a terrible daughter. You should fire me.

GRACE: I saved you some cake.

KATE: Thanks. I wrote a great toast.

GRACE: I'll give you everyone's address. You can send it to them. God, you look exhausted.

KATE: I am so tired.

GRACE: You're going to kill yourself, honey.

KATE: The network will probably beat me to it. They hated this week's script. We were really stuck until Tiffany—why are they always named Tiffany—this twenty-two year-old writer's assistant with very perky boobs and no hips—fixed it. She'll probably be the producer by the end of the season.

GRACE: You think this Tiffany person is after your job?

KATE: I think everyone is. I should be committed. I'm psychotic.

GRACE: Tell me your worst case scenario?

KATE: I lose my job in a dramatic, *career ending* kind of way, get evicted from my apartment, and end up in a greasy overcoat washing windshields at The Lincoln Tunnel—on the Jersey side.

GRACE: Don't be ridiculous. You can always come home and live with us.

KATE: I've reassessed. *That's* my worst case scenario.

GRACE: Katie you make people laugh. That's a gift.

KATE: Stop the presses, call The Times. *(As though reading headline)* UNMARRIED T V PRODUCER GETS LIFE SAVING DOSE OF LOVE FROM MOTHER.

GRACE: You have your health, everything else is attainable. Here. *(Hands KATE a piece of cake)*

KATE: That looks yummy. *(Starts to eat with her fingers)*

GRACE: Katie! Not with your hands.

KATE: Sorry, can I have a fork?

GRACE: *(Suddenly confused)* A what?

KATE: A fork. So I don't look like the barbarian you think I am.

(Off GRACE's blank stare)

KATE: Are you okay? *(No response)* Mom?

GRACE: What? What do you want?

KATE: A fork...?

GRACE: *(Annoyed)* I...I can't find anything in the kitchen. The caterers made a mess. Just eat with your hands.

ACT ONE

KATE: Oookay. It's just with you, neatness usually counts.

GRACE: Honey, stay here tonight. You're too tired to drive.

KATE: I can't.

GRACE: I'll make you a nice breakfast. I'll brush your hair just right into a beautiful upsweep. I have those delicate ivory combs that would make you look so pretty, like a porcelain doll....

KATE: *(Now uncomfortable)* Mom, I have to go.

GRACE: *(Coldly)* So go.

(An uncomfortable silence)

KATE: *(Lifts her glass of champagne)* Happy birthday to my elegant mother. *(Uncomfortable hug)* You know how much I love you.

GRACE: *(Takes plate from KATE)* Go be a success, honey. Don't let anyone stop you. Remember, you're doing it for both of us.

KATE: Yeah. *(Sighs)* No pressure here.

(The lights fade and open on MARTY who talks on phone as a hassled KATE enters.)

MARTY: Don't be silly, you're not bothering her, Mrs Griswald. Kate will be happy to take your call.

(Off KATE's glare)

MARTY: What? She says it's an emergency.

KATE: Hi, Mom. I'm a little rushed. What's up?

GRACE: I haven't seen you for four months.

KATE: Sorry. You know what it's like at the beginning of a series. I'm up to my eyeballs in work. Maybe this weekend or definitely next.

GRACE: *(Frightened)* Katie, how many men live here?

KATE: What do you mean?

GRACE: Some men I don't know have moved in.

KATE: I don't understand. Start from the beginning.

GRACE: I don't know the beginning. I just know there are men I've never seen. Tall, hairy men. Not very good dressers, either. I think they're looking for my money.

KATE: Money? You don't have any. I mean not at home, right?

GRACE: That's what I keep telling them.

KATE: Is Daddy home?

GRACE: Yes.

KATE: *(Looks at watch)* Look, we're pretty light on rewrites. Why don't I come over after I'm done? Say about nine?

GRACE: Thank you, honey. And don't worry if I'm dead.

KATE: *(Startled)* Dead? Do you want me to call the police?

GRACE: *(Alarmed)* Why? What's wrong?

KATE: Mom, let's take this slowly. Are you afraid someone in your house may kill you?

GRACE: The tall one threatened, yes. But I don't think he was serious. Just get here when you can, darling. I'll bake your favorite pie. *(Shakily)* What is it again?

(KATE *holds the phone bewildered for a beat. Looks at the audience)*

KATE: And so it began. Some people don't remember when it happened. When roles started to reverse. But for me there's nothing hazy about it. Some people wrap themselves in repression or denial—I've had my share

ACT ONE

of that. But if a memory marker could be planted, it would be that night.

(KATE *walks into area where* GRACE *and* JACK *are.* GRACE *sits.* JACK *paces.*)

JACK: I keep telling your mother there are no strange men here. *(Like a punch line)* Present company excluded, of course.

GRACE: Everything's a joke to him. Just because *HE* hasn't seen them, it doesn't mean they're not here.

KATE: How could they get in?

GRACE: Keys.

KATE: You lost your keys?

JACK: No!

GRACE: You don't want to tell her, do you?

JACK: *(Escalating anger)* There's nothing to tell.

GRACE: Fine. Pretend it never happened.

KATE: Will one of you please tell me what you're talking about?

(GRACE *mimes zippering her mouth and looks at* JACK.)

JACK: Tell the damn thing. Who cares?

GRACE: Three months ago we parked in this Kinney parking lot and Daddy left the house key on the key ring. I made a little fuss, but he made a bigger fuss so, as always, he did what he wanted. Fifty-two dollar dinner. As much as I enjoyed it, it could've been Alpo. Obviously, those parking people made a copy of the key—I saw that on *Law and Order* once. Now they can get in anytime they please.

JACK: That was three *years* ago, Grace. Not three months.

GRACE: I'll give them demerits for being tardy.

JACK: Do you believe it? This is what I've been living with. *(Angry)* There are no hairy strangers with knives looking for our money.

GRACE: Everyone has a right to his or her own opinion, as the case may be. This is America.

KATE: Why not change the locks?

GRACE: Doesn't matter. They have their ways.

KATE: What ways?

GRACE: How should I know? Do I have a criminal mind?

JACK: Do you hear this? It doesn't stop. She's driving me nuts. Two or three times a day, she goes to check her safe deposit box. The bank wants her to stop coming.

KATE: She can go whenever she wants. Don't worry, Daddy, that one *I'll* take care of.

GRACE: *(As though she has won a point)* Thank you, Katie. Now I want to go to the bank and make sure my money's still there. They've probably cleaned me out.

JACK: The bank is closed.

KATE: Dad's right, Mom. It's almost ten o'clock at night.

GRACE: Why do you always take his side?

KATE: *(Confused)* I don't.

JACK: I need coffee and danish. If only I drank... *(Exits)*

GRACE: Katie, you have to take my journals. I don't want anyone else reading them. Will you do that? Do you promise?

KATE: Yes. Sure.

GRACE: Good. *(Whispering)* Katie. Come here. Close.

(KATE *walks to her mother.*)

ACT ONE 17

GRACE: Do you know who that man is?

KATE: What man?

GRACE: The one who just went out for a danish.

KATE: That's Daddy. Your husband. Jack.

GRACE: *(Covering)* Just checking.

KATE: You don't know he's your husband?

GRACE: *(Lying)* Of course—if you say so. It's just that they all say they're my husband. And they all sound so sincere.

KATE: *(Putting it together)* He's got hairy arms...tall... not exactly a great dresser....

(JACK *walks back in eating a danish.*)

GRACE: *(To unseen man)* I love your jacket, Morton. Such a soft wool. I wish my husband wore something so dashing.

(KATE *and* JACK *look at each other.*)

KATE: Daddy, how long has this been going on?

JACK: It's not always this bad. There are days that she's perfectly fine.

(They walk to GRACE, *coming in on the end of her conversation.)*

GRACE: A lady can dream can't she, Morton?

KATE: Mom, this is Daddy.

GRACE: *(Lucid again)* How long has what been going on?

(KATE *gives her a long look and then walks to the audience and talks.*)

KATE: She would go in and out of being the person I knew. The woman who could finish three crossword puzzles a day, organize a march on Washington, and still fry up juicy Chicken Kiev for dinner. Funny, sharp, stubborn, judgmental. The woman I missed. I knew she had to be examined by a professional.

(Lights up on GRACE *on the phone with* KATE.*)*

GRACE: There is no way I'm seeing a doctor.

KATE: Mother, you parked in the middle of the Lincoln Tunnel.

GRACE: I stopped in front of one of the booths. The man there looked like my Uncle Leo and I wanted to say hello.

KATE: But Uncle Leo is dead.

GRACE: That's why I was so surprised to see him. There will be no doctor. I do not air my dirty linen in public.

KATE: We're just going to find out what the possibilities are.

GRACE: I know from possibilities. Edith what's-her-name died on the operating table. That possibility they told her not to worry about. Okay, so now she's not worrying. Doctors kill you. Show me a person who just died, I'll show you a doctor not ten feet away.

(They walk across the stage.)

KATE: I understand this doctor is a very fine diagnostician. Let's just hear what he suggests.

DOCTOR #1: Three weeks observation in a mental ward.

KATE: *(Looks like he's nuts, to* GRACE*)* We'll move on.

GRACE: I don't want tests. Temma Pearlman had tests. Cancer of something. Two weeks later we were sitting Shiva.

KATE: Don't you know anyone who gets good news?

GRACE: I may. They just don't talk about it.

*(*KATE *and* GRACE *move to another part of the stage.)*

ACT ONE

KATE: Mom, this doctor is a leader in his field. And look at it this way, we are getting to spend time together.

(KATE *and* GRACE *walk to* DOCTOR #2's *office. They sit down.*)

DOCTOR #2: Parkinson's—a mild case. And, of course, Alzheimer's.

KATE: Alzheimer's?

(KATE *looks at* GRACE *and grabs her hand, squeezing it tight.*)

KATE: Just like that you can be so sure?

DOCTOR #2: This *is* my specialty. Of course there's a marginal chance it's just a gradual memory loss. Look at me, dear. What day is today?

GRACE: Monday. *(Beat)* Or, maybe, Friday.

DOCTOR #2: *(Clipped)* Now I'm going to say four words and I want you to repeat them. Train, bus, car, bike.

GRACE: Train...car...bus...was there another?

DOCTOR #2: Now try these. One, three, five... *(Looks at his list)* ...seven.

GRACE: One...I'm not good with numbers.

DOCTOR #2: Who's the mayor of New York, dear?

GRACE: Koch.

(Off KATE's *cough)*

GRACE: No, Dinkins. I read it today.

DOCTOR #2: Do you read much, dear?

GRACE: I used to read more, *dear*. So much more...

DOCTOR #2: Your mother can enroll in our memory program. We drill and test. The cost is two thousand dollars a week. *(Off their gasp)* Of course with

Alzheimer's the only way you can be a hundred percent sure is by doing an autopsy.

KATE: *(Quickly)* We're not *that* curious.

(KATE *and* GRACE *leave his office.*)

(KATE, GRACE *and* JACK *enter the office of* DOCTOR SAM GELMAN, *late thirties, sincere, handsome, genuinely caring. During this scene, he is doing a standard battery of a neurological exam.*)

SAM: Grace—can I call you Grace?

GRACE: I hate when they call me "dear." It makes me feel...I don't remember the word, but that's how it makes me feel.

SAM: Never "dear." So noted. Would you like to call me Sam?

GRACE: Doctor Gelman is fine. I have a hard enough time thinking of someone younger than my shoes as a doctor.

SAM: Fair enough. I'd just like us to be friends. Do you know why I want that?

GRACE: *(Thinks for a moment)* You're desperate for companionship?

SAM: *(Laughs warmly)* Maybe. I hadn't thought of that. No, Grace, it's because friends trust each other. What you're going through isn't easy. Your life is changing. Sometimes confusing; sometimes frightening; sometimes not much different. But the scariest part is not knowing what's happening and what to expect. That's where I'll come in. I'll explain whatever you need to know. And I'll be in your corner. Do you understand what I've said?

GRACE: Well...you're a cute kid, but I know a snow job when I hear one. I think...I think I like you. And hate you.

ACT ONE 21

JACK: Grace.

SAM: No, it's honest. *(Beat)* We're going to need time to build the trust I was talking about.

GRACE: Do you promise I'll never go into a nursing home?

SAM: Not unless it's absolutely necessary.

GRACE: *(Gets up, to* KATE*)* I want to leave.

KATE: Mom, give him a chance.

GRACE: I did. I hate him. He's history. *(Starts to leave)*

SAM: Grace, before you go, I want you to know how impressed I was with all the answers you knew on the test you took.

(GRACE *stops. She turns to look at* SAM.)

GRACE: *(Hopeful again)* Really?

SAM: *(Smiles encouragingly)* Absolutely.

GRACE: *(To* JACK*)* You see. *(Back to* SAM*)* He tried to take away my car keys. Tell him he can't do that.

JACK: *(To* SAM*)* This is the most lucid she's been in months.

GRACE: *(Turning, like a caged animal)* I have to be. I'm fighting for my life. *(A beat)* Every day I'm...slipping.

SAM: I know. There are things we can try. I'll do everything I can to keep you home. I want what you want.

GRACE: You want my daughter to get married, too?

(SAM *laughs.*)

GRACE: Just say you won't put me in a nursing home. *(Beat)* Go ahead. Say it.

SAM: *(Genuinely)* I won't put you in a nursing home.

GRACE: A sincere liar—I appreciate that. Okay, Doctor, I'm yours. *(Snaps fingers)* That question you asked me before—the day after Tuesday? *(Hopefully)* Thursday?

SAM: Close enough.

(GRACE *beams.* JACK *starts to leave with* GRACE.)

KATE: I'll be out in a minute.

(After they exit, to SAM*)*

KATE: So can you help her?

SAM: We've got exciting new drugs on the market. If they work, they stop the patient from slipping as quickly.

KATE: But you're saying she will eventually slip?

SAM: There's no cure yet.

KATE: But you can stop it temporarily, right?

SAM: It's problematic in Grace's case. The drugs used for Parkinson's are often counterproductive for Alzheimer's.

KATE: You hot-shot doctors always have the greatest excuses.

SAM: *(Jarred)* I wasn't expecting you to be hostile. What do you want me to do for your mother, Kate?

KATE: I want you to make her whole again. Your basic miracle.

SAM: I'm working on it. I see by her chart that she didn't respond well to the Tachrine and Donepezil. We can try some of the natural medicines.

KATE: Gingko, Ibuprofen, Vitamin E, C, A. It seemed a little late for hormone replacement.

SAM: No discernible results?

KATE: No. *(Beat)* I'd like a realistic timetable.

ACT ONE

SAM: *(Hedging)* It all depends on the buildup on the platelets. Every case is different.

KATE: I know that. I'm talking specifically about *my mother*. Just give it to me straight.

SAM: What makes your mother potentially resistant to the drugs is the speed of her deterioration. I've never seen a patient go so quickly after the initial onset.

KATE: *(Small ironic laugh)* A record setter. We're so proud. *(Shakes head)* I'm sorry. I don't mean to be hostile. It just hasn't been a four-star year for my family and the medical profession. Will she be able to stay at home?

SAM: Without twenty-four-hour nursing care, probably not. My guess is six months from now she'll be in a nursing home. *(Beat)* Grace put on a show today. Very impressive, but fleeting. She has a rapid progressive degeneration. Her mind is going fast. I doubt she can read anymore. Her concentration will fade. Simple tasks—dressing, brushing her teeth—will become Herculean feats. Her mind will go in and out. Her sentences will be fragments. Sometimes she'll know you, often you'll be a stranger. Her eyes will glaze over. She'll be in an impenetrable world. Physically, she may be fine, live years. Mentally, very little will be left.

(KATE *looks like she has been hit by a nuclear blast.*)

SAM: Can I get you a glass of water? Something to drink?

KATE: Stoli and a straw. *(Beat)* Damn you.

SAM: I'm only the messenger.

KATE: What—you're worried you won't be popular with me?

SAM: I need to have family support.

KATE: You'll have it.

SAM: If it's any consolation, by the time Grace goes, she won't know she's there.

KATE: You don't know my mother.

SAM: But I know this disease. Kate, there's a clinical trial group I can get her in. Would you agree to that?

KATE: Sure. *(Stares into space, ashamed)* I get angry with her. Like it's her fault. Like if she really wanted to, she could do something about it. God, what does that make me?

SAM: Human.

(KATE *walks into her office.* MADGE *is following her.*)

MADGE: I need a bigger dressing room.

KATE: I'll see what I can do.

MADGE: And more money per episode.

KATE: How about a yacht?

MADGE: Hmm... *(Beat)* I assume you saw me in *People* magazine last week? *(Holds up magazine)* "Madge Wellington wows America playing a different waitress every week." Good publicity for the show. *(Beat)* I was thinking I should get a piece of the net. Not a big piece—far be it from me to be piggy. But let's face it—no one could replace me.

KATE: *(Matter-of-fact)* In the sixth year of *Dallas*, when the show was a hot, top-ten property, there was a rumor that Larry Hagman...

MADGE: Lar...

KATE: ...threatened if he didn't get a more obscene amount of money than he was already loading into his Brinks truck, he'd walk. Luckily they had a writer—no Tennessee Williams, but clever—who came up with a solution. Picture it: J R in a car crash. Critical condition. In a coma. Looks hopeless. Just as the heart monitor line is going straight, we hear beep, beep, beep. J R is saved. The viewers heave a collective sigh of relief. Except J R's face is badly burned. Call in a plastic surgeon. The bandages come off. J R returns—but now he has the voice, build and face of... *(Build up)* Robert Culp. *(Beat)* Larry Hagman had a remarkable change of heart.

MADGE: They don't do that in sitcoms.

KATE: Tell that to Valerie Harper.

MADGE: Why the hell are you so damn tough?

KATE: Like my mother used to say, I pay the bills.

MADGE: How long before I can fire the bitch who stands before me?

KATE: End of third season. Mark your calendar.

(KATE *walks into her parents' living room.* GRACE *looks glassy eyed. Throughout the scene* JACK *dresses her and combs her hair.)*

JACK: That's it, sweetheart. You ate a nice lunch today. Look who's here. It's your beautiful daughter.

GRACE: Hello, Gwen.

KATE: Nope. The other one.

GRACE: Hello, darling.

KATE: *(Kissing* GRACE*)* Hello, Mom. How are you today?

GRACE: I'm fine. I think I'm fine. How am I, Jim?

JACK: Jack. My name is Jack. Can you say Jack, Grace?

GRACE: *(Angrily)* Jack.

JACK: Good girl. You look so pretty and you only needed a little help getting dressed. All in all I'd say you're just dandy.

GRACE: *(Repeating)* I'm just dandy.

JACK: Now I'm going to wash these dishes.

KATE: I'll be back. I just want to talk to Daddy for a minute.

GRACE: Just dandy. Mama, look, I'm just dandy.

(KATE *follows* JACK *who is polishing the silver.*)

JACK: *(Sighs)* I brush her teeth, I choose her clothes, yesterday I put on her pantyhose.

KATE: *(Trying to make him laugh)* I don't think you'll fit into her dresses.

JACK: All those "friends" at her party—none of them ever call. Not one. Like they think it's catching.

KATE: Yeah. Charlie is complaining that Mom's Alzheimer's is hurting our social life. You know what Mom said. Only family hangs in there.

JACK: So explain your sister, Gwen, to me. She says it makes her uncomfortable to see her. She doesn't have a good time. *(Shakes head)* A good time. Like if I want her to visit I have to bring in...Cirque de Soleil.

(KATE *talks to the audience.*)

KATE: Every time I saw her a little more had chipped away. *(Beat)* And the doctor's prognosis? My mother went into a nursing home. Seven months to the day after that first prediction. One month for our team. She didn't scream, fight, protest. One life for his team.

(GRACE *is dressed nicely, as always wearing her pearls.* JACK *is with her, holding her hand.* KATE *walks to* GRACE. JACK *takes a small embroidered pillow from the bag and puts it in* GRACE's *hands.*)

KATE: Look at you. Pretty in pink.

JACK: *(Looking at the pillow)* "The Queen lives here".

GRACE: The sun is going to come. I want a piece of....

KATE: Of what, Mom? You want a piece of what?

ACT ONE

JACK: She can't hold on to a thought anymore.
Her mind is a sieve. It kills me to see her like this.

KATE: Oh, Daddy...

JACK: She stares into space. We sit and say nothing.
Your mother saying nothing. Can you imagine?
She hated when there was silence. I used to say, Grace,
take a breath. We don't always have to be talking.
But she thought it showed a lack of intelligence if there
wasn't conversation. She was a spellbinder. Me, I could
tell jokes, sure, but her, she was something. She was
going to change the world. Now she just sits here
empty. She doesn't know who I am. *(To* GRACE*)* Say
Jack. Say hello, Jack. *(Defeated)* Not even who I am...

KATE: Why don't you go home? You look so tired.

JACK: The house is empty.

KATE: So sell it.

JACK: The house is the only thing the government won't
take from you to pay for this. No Medicaid until I'm
broke. I checked. Fifty-five thousand a year this costs.

KATE: I told you I could help.

JACK: *(Angry)* I don't want your help. I'm just
answering your question. *(Calms down)* I'm going nuts.
I swear, she's not the only one suffering here.

KATE: You need a vacation.

JACK: I could also use a full head of hair. I don't think
either's going to happen.

KATE: Daddy, I'm not kidding. You have to get away.

JACK: How? I can't leave your mother. Look at her.

KATE: I'll come here more often; I'll hire additional
help. You deserve a break. Why don't you go to Miami?

JACK: Yeah, there's a real shortage of old Jewish men there.

KATE: Don't you usually go to a Dental Convention around now?

JACK: Yeah, I just threw out the notice.

KATE: You're no good to Mom like this. You need some R&R. Please.

JACK: *(Thinking)* Okay, I'll go. Maybe I'll see some familiar mouths. *(Exits)*

(SAM enters, but says nothing. He watches KATE with GRACE.)

GRACE: Did Papa go?

KATE: Daddy will be back later. *(Realizing)* Oh, Papa—you mean your Papa? Was he here again?

GRACE: He comes to bring chocolates. He loves me, you know.

KATE: I know. Who could blame him?

(KATE kneels by GRACE and gently kisses her hand.)

KATE: You know I love you.

GRACE: *(Tears in her eyes)* How can you?

KATE: Because you're my mother. *(Beat)* I wish we could travel cross-country. We could go to the Grand Canyon. Just the two of us. Wouldn't that be fun?

GRACE: *(In another world)* The shoes don't have pancakes. I know it would be seven....

(KATE sees GRACE is gone now. SAM clears his throat so KATE will know he's there.)

SAM: Well, hello. How are you?

KATE: Me, I'm fine. But then *I'm* not your patient.

SAM: I'm sorry she didn't respond to the clinical trial.

ACT ONE

KATE: That's okay. Somebody had to get the placebo.

SAM: You really write comedy? Is it black?

KATE: No, I haven't covered the medical profession yet.

SAM: Sorry, I don't watch television.

KATE: Yeah, well, everyone I meet spends his evenings either soaking up N P R or re-reading Kissinger's memoirs. God knows where we pick up twenty million viewers.

SAM: What's it called?

KATE: "Order Up!" Wednesday nights, nine o'clock. Be there.

SAM: I'll try to watch it, okay?

KATE: Okay. Are you a Nielsen household?

SAM: Maybe. What if I were?

KATE: I'd have to be nice to you.

SAM: Would that include letting me take you to dinner?

KATE: Are you kidding? I'd sleep with you.

SAM: I only asked you for dinner.

KATE: So fucking is out?

(SAM *looks embarrassed.*)

KATE: Great—I'm being hypothetically rejected. *(Beat)* Welcome to my life.

(KATE's *cell phone rings.*)

KATE: Kate Griswald. *(Beat)* Jeez, Marty, what now?

SAM: *(Walks to* GRACE*)* Hi, Grace. It's Sam. How are you today?

GRACE: Uncle Lou likes my coat. The dog's outside.

KATE: Because then the setup in act one goes out the window. Bullshit. Don't screw it up. That's *my* job.
(To SAM*)* Hey, Doc, what's funnier, cupcake or cookie?

SAM: *(Considers)* Cupcake.

KATE: *(On phone)* Go with cupcake. *(Hangs up)*

SAM: Trouble delegating responsibility?

KATE: Not as long as I give it all to me.

SAM: Grace, you've got one hard-nosed daughter there.

KATE: And what kind of a *mother* do I have?

SAM: A sweetheart.

KATE: Yeah, she is that. Not critical anymore. Another one of life's ironies.

SAM: *(Surprised)* Grace was critical?

KATE: I survived. So, when are you going to work your miracle on her?

SAM: Give me a little time.

KATE: I believe we're running low on that commodity.

SAM: We'll see. In the meantime, how about dinner?

KATE: I've got to get back to the studio.

SAM: How about tomorrow night?

KATE: We tape two shows. You're a persistent one.

SAM: I want to see if I can win at least one round with you.

KATE: I'm a challenge, huh? Really gets that old testosterone going. Sorry, I don't have time for a relationship. If I did, there's one I'm rather skillfully ignoring.

(MADGE *appears rehearsing, while* KATE *and* SAM *walk to a table being set up in a restaurant.)*

ACT ONE

MADGE: *(Rehearsing lines in Japanese)* Dumo...Dumo? Domo. Domo Arigato. Domo arigato gazayamasta. *(Repeats several times)* I'm not wearing these freakin' shoes! Wardrobe!

SAM: ...And I was fourteen when my Grandpa Al died. They called it senility back then. This indomitable man had made me the center of his universe. When he disappeared into Alzheimer's, I knew what my life's work was going to be. Funny how events choose you. *(Looks at* KATE*)* What? I'm boring you, right? We spend a whole evening talking about me. Typical male.

KATE: And then I realize you don't even know my name, much less if you want to see me again and then I pick up the check.

SAM: Kate. I want to. And I'm paying.

KATE: You bring up the curve. I wasn't bored. I was... jealous. You really love your work.

SAM: You love your work.

KATE: It's different. There's a tangible value to what you do. This is strange for me to say. I don't particularly like doctors.

SAM: You hide it well.

KATE: I think you could make a difference. Make a believer out of me, Sam.

SAM: I'm trying. So tell me about Kate.

KATE: There are eight million stories in The Naked City...Kate's just one of them.

SAM: But she's at my table. So I'm curious. Why haven't you ever gotten married?

KATE: Did my mother send you?

SAM: Really. You're pretty, smart, witty.

KATE: Yes, I'm definitely the eighth wonder of the world. Okay, let's see, well, it wasn't because I was never asked because I was. Surprised?

SAM: No.

KATE: Brad Sanger. A really nice guy, you know. Well, for a standup comedian, which means he's basically a neurotic exposed nerve. *(Shrugs)* It just didn't work out. I was busy meeting a deadline and forgot to show up at City Hall. Can you believe that? I was a cad. I left Brad standing at the municipal altar. He said it was a bad sign. But I figure if you can't fit in time to elope it probably isn't kismet.

SAM: You didn't answer my question.

KATE: *(Thinking)* I guess I haven't gotten married because my mother wants it too much.

SAM: I'm serious.

KATE: So am I.

(KATE's *cell phone rings.*)

KATE: Kate Griswald. Oh my god, Charlie, I completely forgot. I'm here with my mother's doctor. *(Whispers to* SAM*)* My semi-significant other. *(Back to* CHARLIE*)* I know it's late for a consultation, but this is a very...dedicated...doctor.

(KATE *reenters, carrying a journal and photo album. It is a different day.*)

KATE: I'm discovering all sorts of things about you in your journal, Mom. Did you know you were once an optimist? Oh, no, look at this. You've touched up every one of these pictures. Except gaw-jess Gwen, of course. Oh, God, you erased your nose in this one.

(JACK *enters, wearing a Hawaiian shirt and white ducks. He sneaks up behind* KATE, *and puts his hands over her eyes.*)

ACT ONE

JACK: *(Low voice)* Guess who?

KATE: Bea Arthur. *(Turning around)* My god, what a tan. You look great. Ten, maybe twenty years younger. Mom, look, it's Don Ho.

JACK: *(Kisses GRACE)* Hi, honey. Miss me?

GRACE: The cat forgot his galoshes.

KATE: So, tell me about your trip.

JACK: I played golf, volleyball. My jokes were a hit.

KATE: I bet you made tons of friends.

JACK: One special one. We had a wonderful time together.

KATE: After the last fifteen months, you deserve it.

JACK: What a relief to hear you say that. I told Lorna you'd want me to be happy.

KATE: *(Realizing)* Lorna? Like the guy on "Bonanza"?

JACK: No, that was Lorne. Lorne Greene. This is Lorna. You're going to love her. She's perfect. I mean, I got so lucky.

KATE: *(Trying to be restrained)* Lucky. Really? So, how did you meet this Lorna person?

JACK: Miami's like the dating game. There must be a tote board somewhere. *(As though reading the board)* Single man with pulse enters State. *(Pulling arm of an invisible jackpot machine)* Ka-ching, ka-ching.

KATE: Hardly single.

JACK: We took pina colada soap showers together. I've never been so... clean.

KATE: Gee, I'm so proud.

JACK: Kate, we have so much in common. One night Lorna comes to my hotel room with a pastrami sandwich. Extra lean. Just like I order. Isn't that uncanny?

KATE: Oh, yeah, especially considering all the people ordering it with extra fat.

JACK: I want to spend my life with her.

KATE: I hate to put a damper on "Love Comes to Andy Hardy", but do you notice, maybe, something wrong with this picture? *(She looks at* GRACE.*)*

JACK: Your mother is my number one girl. But look at her. She doesn't know me. What's my name, Grace? Who am I?

(GRACE *looks glassy eyed.*)

KATE: Stop it. You know she can't answer questions like that.

JACK: That's as good as it'll ever be. You think otherwise, you're kidding yourself. She's as good as gone.

KATE: Daddy, not in front of her.

JACK: *(Furious)* Nothing. She understands nothing! Who am I, Grace? Am I your husband... your brother? She's a blank slate. Can't you see that? *(Calms down)* It's not like I'd divorce her. That's unconscionable. But I need a life, too. I thought you, of all people, would understand.

KATE: You want absolution, find a priest.

JACK: You think I planned this? Miami was *your* idea.

KATE: Thanks. I was running low on guilt.

JACK: It just happened, that's all. I told Lorna about your mother. She's willing to hang in. She loves me. Besides, she has time; she's only fifty-two.

KATE: Fifty-two? She knows your age?

ACT ONE

JACK: *(Hedging)* It's possible she thinks I'm a little younger. Maybe five or twelve years.

(KATE's *cell phone rings.*)

KATE: Kate Griswald. Yes. *(Beat)* Okay, I'm on my way. *(Hangs up)*

JACK: *(Pointedly)* We all have lives to live, Kate. *(Beat)* For the first time in years, I'm happy to get up in the morning. *(Beat)* It's not easy. We all need questions answered. Like the meaning of life...like what the future holds...like how many times a night a woman can have an orgasm?

KATE: *(Shocked)* Excuse me?

JACK: *(Sheepishly)* I was just wondering. You know, on the average.

KATE: *(A beat)* Twenty-four.

(JACK *looks stricken.*

KATE: *(Turns, to audience)* I figure he goes, he goes.

(KATE *pulls out her cell phone, talking on it.)*

KATE: Look, Gwen, he sees Mom all the time—unless he's in Miami. Well, how *would* you know, you're never here? Say, weren't you supposed to be the good daughter? It'd be nice if you made a little effort to keep the title. *(Beat)* Yes, tonight, we discussed this... So I guess I'll be there alone when Lorna rides into the Ponderosa.

(KATE *walks into a restaurant where* JACK *and* LORNA, *fifties, built, sweet, are sitting. She and* JACK *are lovey-dovey throughout as a waiter brings dishes and reacts.)*

JACK: I told Kate how you knew her name even before we met.

LORNA: It's true. I'm one of those people who read credits. Probably because I was sort of in show business.

JACK: Lorna was the lead role on Broadway in "Fiddler".

LORNA: I wasn't the lead, sweetie. I played Hodel. *(Beat)* A long time ago. *(Beat)* Back in Cincinnati. *(Beat)* At the Y.

JACK: The "Broadway of Ohio." Lorna moved from Cincinnati to Miami after her husband died.

LORNA: I needed to get away from those memories. Anyway, I want you to know I never miss your show. I'm such a fan.

KATE: Thanks.

LORNA: I just adore that Madge Wellington. What's she really like in real life?

KATE: On a good day...a bitch.

LORNA: *(Gasps)* Really? But she seems like such a sweet person.

KATE: It's called acting.

JACK: You two are going to get along like gangbusters. Did I tell you that Lorna knew your name before she met me?

KATE: Yes. She's a credits reader.

LORNA: Kate, dear, I know how hard this must be on you. Jackie tells me how close you and your mother were.

KATE: *Are*. She's not dead.

LORNA: Oh-my-God, I'm sorry, how insensitive of me. I know this is painful. I remember how hard it was when my mother was dying. She choked to death on a piece of flank steak.

(KATE *looks at her like she's a loon.*)

ACT ONE

JACK: So there I was sitting at this gingivitis luncheon and who do you think sits down next to me?

KATE: Wild guess—Lorna?

LORNA: It was fate. I mean, I wasn't even supposed to be there.

KATE: You were at a bleeding gums luncheon on spec?

JACK: She sat down and that was it. Puss pockets, oral surgery—I didn't hear a word of it.

LORNA: It was embarrassing. I was trying to listen to the speaker and your father here is fondling me.

KATE: Fondling? This part you omitted.

JACK: I couldn't keep my hands off her. As though some magnetic force had come over me.

LORNA: It's like those animals. You know how they sniff around and then urinate so they can stake their territory? It was like Jackie was making his claim—without the urine.

KATE: His manners are impeccable that way.

LORNA: I tried to stop him, but there's no stopping Jackie when he's determined. After lunch we went for a stroll on the boardwalk. I mean, what else could I do?

KATE: 9-1-1 comes to mind.

LORNA: And chance losing this cutie? Never ever.

(KATE's *cell phone rings.*)

KATE: Marty, you should see her. She's like Doris Day without the virginity. And bazooms that don't end. I swear, she does jumping jacks, she'll knock herself unconscious. They can't keep their hands off each other. One time he kissed her, I thought he was in there for the night.

(KATE *clicks off the cell,* JACK & LORNA *are snuggling and growling at each other.* KATE *is uncomfortable.*)

KATE: Okay, you two. Another round? Or shall I just send it up with room service?

LORNA: Oh, forgive me. *Quel faux pas.* It's just when we're in each other's company we just get so...

JACK/LORNA: ...involved.

LORNA: We're soulmates.

JACK: *(Friskily)* And playmates...

LORNA: Did your daddy tell you about the time we were in the Poconos? We had this fabulous Jacuzzi....

KATE: Check, please!

LORNA: So Jack's in the Jacuzzi and the man in the bathroom downstairs calls complaining water's leaking on his head while he's on the can. So I rush into the bathroom and—get this—the Jacuzzi spigots are pointed up and there's Jackie, poor baby, spread eagle trying to stop the water.

(LORNA *and* JACK *laugh.*)

KATE: Oh, there's a visual I needed.

JACK: Say, did I tell you this one: Guy walks into a bar with a duck on his head. Bartender says "can I help you?" The duck says "Yeah, can you get this guy off my butt?"

LORNA: *(Laughs appreciatively)* Oh, Jackie, stop. Your father slays me. It's like living with Henny Youngman. *(Immediate turn)* By the way, I love your earrings. Are they real?

KATE: Yes. My mother gave them to me. She has exquisite taste.

ACT ONE   39

LORNA: I could see that. I mean, I love the decor of the house.

KATE: Like my mother—understated elegance.

LORNA: I agree. Very classical. Straight from a Robin Leach special. I can rest you assured, I'll hardly change a thing after we're married.

KATE: Excuse me?

JACK: *(Sheepishly)* I guess I forgot to mention, Kate. Lorna and I are getting married.

KATE: Not unless you move to Utah. Bigamy is still a crime here. Florida, too, I'll bet.

JACK: I filed for a divorce.

LORNA: I'm going to find the little girl's room and tinkle.

(She exits. KATE *waits until* LORNA *exits, seething.)*

KATE: *(Loathingly)* Suddenly this became conscionable?

JACK: Practical. Otherwise, the government ends up with all the money I worked so hard to save.

KATE: You mean you and *Mom* worked so hard to save.

JACK: Everyone does it. Why should I be the only shmuck in America?

KATE: You think a shmuck is only defined economically?

JACK: Kate, I'm in love.

KATE: No. You're in heat. I understand that. But you've been married to Mom for forty-two years.

JACK: I was never in love with Grace like this. Lorna's perfect and she thinks I am, too.

KATE: Of course. You have clean slates. You haven't seen overwhelmed with babies. She hasn't seen losing it over bills. So now, when you can finally relax, it's with a person who hasn't seen you fail.

JACK: Don't start with this guilt trip.

KATE: You should feel guilty. Mom's not an economic loophole; she's your wife. Forty-two years should count for more than a disposable inconvenience. Damn it, you owe her. Shame on you.

JACK: I'll still go to see Grace. Lorna knows how devoted I am to your mother.

KATE: Yeah. I'd pay close attention to that if I were Lorna.

(There is silence.)

JACK: *(Trying to lessen the tension)* Did I tell you the one about Celine Dion walking into a bar? Bartender says, "Hey, Celine, why the long face?"

(Trying to explain the joke to a stone-faced KATE*)*

JACK: Celine Dion has this real long face like a horse....

(KATE *walks from the table into* GRACE's *room.* SAM *is there.)*

SAM: Hi. You look awful.

KATE: Is this a medical or cosmetic opinion? Because if it's cosmetic, I'm going to find a scalpel and stab you.

SAM: In that case, medical.

KATE: In that case, prescribe something. Valium would be nice. Thorazine would be better.

SAM: Kate, I think I have the drug that could reverse Grace's condition.

KATE: How, she doesn't even talk anymore?

SAM: It's called Prolox. It's an experimental drug. But it takes into account both the nerve growth factor and

ACT ONE

insulin-like growth factor so it's not only neuroprotective, but also has the unusual ability to rescue nerve cells from beta amyloid toxicity.

KATE: Oh, God, I actually understand what you're saying.

SAM: It's early, but I've had unprecedented success with laboratory mice who responded...

KATE: *(Interrupting)* Mice? What, they were forgetting their times tables and now they're doing square roots? Forget it. I've been down this road. I'm not sacrificing my mother to science anymore. Get someone on death row.

SAM: Is there a quality of life there you think I'd be tampering with? What is it you're holding on to?

KATE: Every breath she takes, damn it. She knows me. I'm not saying she knows my name. That's gone. But in her way she loves me. She remembers that. I can feel it.

SAM: I think she's an excellent candidate.

KATE: *(Beat)* Convince me.

SAM: Alzheimer's has seven stages. By stage five, the plaque on the brain has triggered such a vast inflammatory reaction, it has killed too many innocent cells to recover.

KATE: My mother *is* in stage five.

SAM: No. Now I'm convinced that Grace is only in stage three.

KATE: But look at her. She has all the symptoms of stage five.

SAM: That's what fooled us. Her rapid progression camouflaged the reality and, ultimately, I believe, the possibilities.

KATE: So the fact that she's going so fast...

SAM: *(Finishing her thought)* ...may actually be working for her now.

KATE: You've taken a new CAT scan?

SAM: *(Shakes his head yes)* It shows an abundance of viable brain cells. Her health is great. Best of all, she's a fighter.

KATE: So this is a cure?

SAM: No, there is no cure yet. It would be a reversal.

KATE: *(Thinks a beat)* How long will it last?

SAM: That's what we'll find out.

KATE: I need time to think about it.

SAM: If you don't give her a chance NOW, it's over. That woman's struggling to get out, but she can't do it without your help.

(KATE *goes to* GRACE *and looks carefully at her.*)

KATE: What do I have to do?

SAM: I need the family's consent.

KATE: I have Power of Attorney.

SAM: You'd also have to sign an agreement that we could study her progress.

KATE: She'd have to stay here.

SAM: She's our research. I had to beg for extra funding. So, how about it? One small step for peoplekind?

KATE: *(Patting* GRACE's *face)* So, what do you think? You always said not to quit. Mom, remember how you said Morton Seligman told you to learn to risk? *(To* SAM*)* She looks so tired. *(Beat)* Mom, you know how much I love you.

GRACE: I love you... *(Forcing out the name)* ...Katie.

(KATE *looks up, almost not believing she has heard* GRACE *say her name.* KATE *looks at* SAM. *What* SAM *has said now makes sense to her.*)

KATE: When do we begin?

END ACT ONE

ACT TWO

(A different set of doctored pictures of KATE *appears as light comes up.)*

KATE: So as it turns out once again, medicine isn't an exact science. Two months and nothing. No change. Status quo. Then again, the rest of my life wasn't exactly *The Sound of Music* either.

*(*KATE *pushes her answering machine. A beep sounds. The message says, "You have nineteen messages."* JACK *and* LORNA *appear in a pool of light, all bubbly and snuggly.)*

JACK: Kate, we just called to tell you that we were looking at wedding invitations today.

LORNA: We were thinking of a theme wedding. Wouldn't that be oodles of fun? Lovers living and dead. What do you think?

JACK: I could be Romeo.

LORNA: And I could be Cleopatra.

(A second beep sounds. Another pool of light shines on MADGE.*)*

MADGE: Did you see our ratings this week? We're losing to re-runs of Mister Ed.

(The light goes off. KATE *walks into* GRACE*'s room.* SAM *is examining* GRACE *who sits in the wheelchair, glassy eyed.* GRACE*'s head now slips to one side. Her appearance is more deteriorated.)*

KATE: So, did I miss any miracles today?

SAM: Patience. It's a virtue.

KATE: I'm an immediate gratification person. To me, success is a virtue. *(Looks at* GRACE*)* So, how's the main event?

SAM: Sometimes I think she hears me.

KATE: Sometimes I believe in God. Usually just before they announce the winners at the Emmys. Give me tangibles.

SAM: The other day for a flash she looked like the old Grace, struggling to get through.

KATE: Mom, it's Kate. *(No response)* She hardly moves anymore. Where are her pearls? I told the nurses my mother always wears pearls. She's a lady. *(Puts on* GRACE's *pearls angrily)* Look at her. She's a zombie. I want you to stop the Prolox. *(Rummages through her purse, pulls out a pack of cigarettes and lights up)*

SAM: I can adjust the dosage.

KATE: I'm taking back my consent.

SAM: You signed an agreement.

KATE: Sue me. *(Heads for the door)*

GRACE: Katie.

(KATE *stops and turns around.*)

GRACE: Those cigarettes will kill you.

(KATE *and* SAM *react.*)

(KATE *is on her cell. A pool of light on* JACK.)

JACK: You know how you exaggerate.

KATE: No, Daddy, that's *you*.

JACK: Then she's completely well?

KATE: I'm not saying she's perfect. But she's on her way. Every day there's some improvement. It's only been a month. You've got to have patience. *(Turns to the audience)* It's a word I just added to my vocabulary.

(KATE *walks into* GRACE's *room.* GRACE *wears a robe and slippers. Still not a hundred percent, she looks better.)*

KATE: You look gorgeous.

GRACE: Gorgeous I don't look. You get me an appointment at Lizbess Charden's, then we'll talk.

KATE: You mean Elizabeth Arden?

GRACE: Elizabeth Arden... *(Beat)* This gray is for old ladies. I need something jazzy. Maybe ass blond.

KATE: Ash, Mom. Ash.

(SAM *enters.)*

SAM: Well, I see you've got yourself a visitor, Grace.

GRACE: It's my daughter, Katie, back again. But then you already know her, don't you?

SAM: You know, Grace, Kate and I have had dinner.

GRACE: Oh, right, but she really only wanted to fuck.

KATE: *(Shocked)* Mother. Language.

GRACE: You mean "fuck"? It was a direct quote. Besides, it's just a word. Fuck, fuck, fuck. I like it.

KATE: Wait a second. You heard things said in front of you?

GRACE: And some behind my back, too.

(SAM *and* KATE *walk out together.)*

SAM: She's making incredible progress.

KATE: Progress? As my father would say, better than poi-fect.

SAM: She's on her way. She needs help with words. I'm not trying to diminish how far she's come.

KATE: Seems to me you're hoarding those gold stars, Doc.

SAM: Nothing I say comes out right with you, no matter how hard I try.

KATE: Try harder.

SAM: Grace was right about one thing. *(Looks intently at* KATE*)* You've been in my head ever since we had dinner together.

KATE: You're sure it was me? I have one of those faces.

SAM: Do you ever let up on yourself?

KATE: Hey, I know I'm destined for greatness. I'm just pacing myself.

SAM: You're so self-deprecating.

KATE: As though insight ever changes anything. Listen, Doc, I'm not a long-term investment. Sooner or later one of us will get hurt. My track record says "sooner."

SAM: Thanks for the disclaimer. Well, obviously you haven't thought about me.

KATE: *(Is he kidding)* Maybe once or twice. So I guess fucking isn't out.

SAM: I do not fuck. I make love.

KATE: Okay, I've got forty-five minutes.

SAM: Usually I like to have a few dinners, good wine, talk, get to know a woman before I make love to her.

KATE: You're too kinky for me. Look, I can't possibly be your type. I'm a fast-talking, neurotic workaholic.

SAM: Yeah, I'm generally attracted to slow-witted, placid underachievers.

ACT TWO

KATE: I see you with someone neutral with a perpetual smile. Maybe Tipper Gore has a sister. *(Off his smile)* So you like me, huh?

SAM: Watching your compassion with Grace—I think it's a dimension you don't even know you have.

KATE: There's nothing that turns a woman on more than talking about her mother. I mean are we into foreplay here?

SAM: Kate, I'm not interested in being some meaningless one-night stand....

KATE: Hey, I try not to get my hopes *that* high.

SAM: Will you please listen to me for a minute without interrupting? *(She mimes zipping her lips.)* If by some great stretch of the imagination we do end up in bed—*(Slowly)* you may be "fucking" me, but I'll be making love to you. And when we're done, I promise you, you'll know the difference.

(KATE *is mesmerized. The light shines on her as she takes in the feelings. Smiling, she walks into her office.*)

MARTY: Now just don't have a hissy fit.

KATE: This can never be good news.

MARTY: *(Hands her newspaper)* Charlie got married.

KATE: Oh, my God. I'm an ex-girlfriend on *Page Six*. He didn't even have the decency to call me. That bastard.

MARTY: The worst. I'm on record I never liked him. And look at her. What a bow wow. She definitely needs work.

KATE: *(Appreciative)* Thank you.

MARTY: I've ordered a dartboard with his picture in the middle. Oh, by the way, Madge is on her way up. We've dropped out of the top twenty.

(MADGE *enters, near hysteria.*)

MADGE: *(Booming drama)* We're doomed. I just bought a condo in Beaver Creek. I barely bargained. Those thieves.

(KATE *pours* MADGE *a glass of wine.*)

KATE: Calm down. Now take a sip of wine.

(KATE *hands* MADGE *the glass.*)

MADGE: *(As she drinks)* I hired a decorator. He did Madonna's castle.

KATE: That's it. One more sip. Thata girl.

MADGE: He was in *Architectural Digest*. A five-page spread. Should I fire him? Should I fire him? I feel a stroke coming on.

(KATE *re-fills the glass.*)

KATE: Don't fire him. The same thing happened on *(Thinking quickly)* Frasier, Friends...

MADGE: *Seinfeld*?

KATE: *Seinfeld.* The network is totally behind us. Order another wing.

MADGE: *Will and Grace*?

KATE: *Will and Grace.*

(MADGE *exits. To* MARTY)

KATE: We're in the toilet.

MARTY: Where are you going?

KATE: To see my mother. She's the positive news in my life.

MARTY: And you're leaving me with Cruella DeVille?

(KATE *walks to* GRACE's *room.* GRACE *is packing a suitcase.*)

KATE: Mom, what are you doing?

ACT TWO

GRACE: Packing.

KATE: Why are you packing?

GRACE: *(Deadpan)* For my talent portion of The Miss America Contest.

KATE: I'm serious.

GRACE: I'm packing because I'm leaving.

KATE: What? Does Sam know about this?

GRACE: All I am is his little white mouse.

KATE: Sam has to record your progress.

GRACE: Ever heard of A T & T? Let him reach out and touch me.

KATE: We signed a contract.

GRACE: *(Slams the suitcase shut)* Not *me*.

KATE: I'm scared something could happen to you.

GRACE: I'm scared nothing will. Everything was always for you or your sister or your father. That's over. Death doesn't scare me. I've been living it for two years. Please, Katie, for once be my friend.

(SAM *enters.*)

SAM: You can't leave. We talked about this this morning. We have to monitor you closely. *(To* KATE*)* Aren't you going to say something to her?

(Off KATE's *shrugs)*

SAM: Suddenly you've become nonverbal?

KATE: *(Weakly)* I told her not to go.

GRACE: It's *my* decision. I'm voting age. Katie, tell your friend he's a rotten control freak.

(SAM *storms out.*)

KATE: *(To* GRACE*)* Stay put! *(Runs after* SAM*)* Sam.

SAM: *(Furious)* And you! Where is your head? Do you know the high odds of liver damage or any number of medical complications?

KATE: All she wants to do is to go home. She'll be available to you. She's not stupid.

SAM: The board won't permit drugs as an outpatient. The whole pilot program goes down the drain.

KATE: Sam, she has a right to have a life.

SAM: Which she wouldn't have if I hadn't pushed her to the front of the line.

KATE: So if you give someone a heart transplant, they're yours for life?

SAM: Four million people have Alzheimer's, in twenty years, triple that. Grace is the only ammunition we have right now. Don't you see the importance of that?

KATE: You're talking about numbers, Sam. I'm talking about my mother.

SAM: This *is* for your mother. And you. One out of every two children of Alzheimer's victims is genetically prone to getting this disease.

KATE: I feel really bad for Gwen.

SAM: She'll regress immediately. She won't have any medicine.

KATE: *(Slowly)* She'll have medicine.

SAM: Exactly how is that going to happen?

KATE: *(Gently)* Because you'll give it to her. That Hippocratic Oath has value for you. You care about every individual. I envy that. It's what I admire about you. And it's what's going to keep my mother alive.

SAM: Then respect who I am and what I'm trying to do.

ACT TWO 53

(SAM *turns and leaves.* KATE *walks to* GRACE's *room.* GRACE *is on the phone.*)

GRACE: I'll pick up the tickets in half an hour. (*Hangs up*)

KATE: What tickets?

GRACE: To go cross-country to the Grand Canyon like you said. I could stop off in Chicago to see Morton Seligman. Then I'd like to drop by Florida and shoot your father in the heart.

KATE: Mom, I just promised Sam you'd stay available.

GRACE: Only make promises you can keep. Okay, we leave tomorrow.

KATE: *We*? I've got an important job.

GRACE: Writing punch lines, Katie. I mean, let's face it, you're not exactly Arthur Miller. Quit.

KATE: Quit??! There's no way I'm going to.... I've worked years to get... I don't even have time to have this argument. Mom, if I leave this job I'm out of a career. Who are you? My mother would never do this to me. The timing is all wrong. The network is talking about giving me an overall deal. My show's in trouble. They need me. They need me.

GRACE: So do I, Katie. (*Beat*) I've never said that before. I always thought, when I really need Katie, she'll do it because it's right, not because she's guilted into.

KATE: Oh god, you're using reverse guilt.

GRACE: How many people would give anything to have their mother back? When you think about it, I'm giving you a gift.

KATE: If you leave, Sam will never talk to me again. Mom, (*Her ace*) he could be the father of your unborn grandchildren.

GRACE: (*Shrugs*) There'll be others.

KATE: I don't believe you. You channel me into a career, you tell me to find Mister Right and now I could lose both. The only way to please you is to fail. And we both know *that* won't please you.

GRACE: Remind me to enter this in my journal.

KATE: Mother, focus.

GRACE: Oh, I am focused, dear. It just took me sixty-six years to do it. Now *you* focus. I'm not staying here because you have a good show or a cute suitor. That self-sacrifice thing has lost its appeal.

KATE: You're going on a kamikaze mission and asking me to be your copilot.

GRACE: You are such a drama queen. I'm going, end of discussion. I'd love you with me. Frankly, I thought you were the only one with me this whole journey. You surprised me there. But if you can't come, I'll manage. Like you always say, we do what we have to.

KATE: *(Thinks a minute)* One week.

GRACE: You're negotiating with me?

KATE: No, I'm making you a final offer.

GRACE: Three months.

KATE: One week.

GRACE: Two months.

KATE: One week.

GRACE: Two weeks and—no argument—I'll come back. I promise on my life.

KATE: Promise on *my* life. Your life doesn't seem to be worth too much to you.

GRACE: Oh, you couldn't be more wrong about that, my love.

ACT TWO

(GRACE *exits and gives sweater to* KATE. KATE *takes out her cell and talks to* MARTY.)

MARTY: I hate to put a kibosh on your trip to the Grand Canyon....

KATE: *(Interrupting)* You know what? I've actually perfected balancing my laptop on the back of a donkey.

MARTY: It's official, the network is moving us to Saturday night.

KATE: You must be joking. No one will find us. Why don't they just put the show on a milk carton?!

MARTY: On the sunny side, the new desk you ordered is finally here. The rosewood is lovely.

KATE: Oh, great, I wait over a year and they deliver the wrong one. I ordered a deep mahogany.

MARTY: *(Looks at bill)* No, it specifically says, "light rosewood because it will brighten my daughter's complexion."

KATE: *(Angrily punching in new number on cell)* I don't believe it. The woman was nearly comatose and she was still in charge. *(Now on different call, waiting)* Oh, goody, the answering machine again. We're getting to be close pals. Sam, I think you should fire this machine because it obviously isn't giving you messages that I've called. C'mon, Sam, call me back. She's really doing fine. I could tell you personally if...

(The phone beeps, KATE *looks at phone)*

KATE: Oh, beep you. *(She starts typing on her laptop.)*

*(*GRACE *stands downstage. She looks out at the view.)*

GRACE: HELLO!

(The canyon echoes her words: "Hello-hello—Hello-lo-lo-lo")

GRACE: Grace is gorgeous!

(The canyon echoes her words: "Grace is gorgeous! Grace is gorgeous! is gorgeous! gorgeous!")

GRACE: Sale at Saks!

(The canyon echoes: "Saks-Saks-Saks-Saks-Saks."
GRACE *sighs a long almost orgasmic satisfied sigh.)*

GRACE: Hi. Want to be my date tonight for a chick flick?

KATE: *(An edge)* No, I'm really not in the chick flick mood right now. My show has been moved to Saturday night and the doctor I thought I was dating won't return my calls. So it seems that he has DUMPED ME!

(The canyon echoes: "DUMPED ME! DUMPED ME! DUMPED ME!")

GRACE: Oh, c'mon, they're showing Bogey and Bacall. *(Singing)* Forget your troubles come on get happy...

KATE: You are such a romantic. I don't get it. It's not like your love ever paid off at the bank.

GRACE: *(Stung)* Whoa. You're a romance capitalist, darling. Every time your emotional investment dips, you sell your stock.

KATE: Disappointment doesn't appeal to me.

GRACE: No one embraces it, Katie. You're so strong in your professional life, but when it comes to your personal life you're Jell-O. You never take personal risks.

KATE: Gee, I wonder where I learned that?

GRACE: I had reasons. You, you're smart, pretty....

KATE: Which would explain why you always touch up my photos.

GRACE: You always took these things wrong.

KATE: You never changed Gwen's pictures.

GRACE: What could I do—white out her brain?

KATE: You honestly don't know how critical of me you are?

GRACE: I never criticize you.

KATE: What did you say when I got this sitcom job?

GRACE: I don't know. Congratulations? Who remembers?

KATE: You said, and I quote, "Why didn't they give you a drama to write?"

GRACE: It was a question.

KATE: No, it was a statement *disguised* as a question. You were saying my work wasn't serious enough.

GRACE: I'm sure Doestoyevsky's mother wanted him to write comedy. This is silly. Ask anyone how I can't stop bragging about my daughter.

KATE: Oh, right, that's me. Miss Fashion Impaired. The one you're always telling how to dress.

GRACE: Can I help it if I'm blessed with a flair for fashion?

KATE: The only "flair" you didn't have was academics. Thank God I had somewhere to escape. Even now there are times with you I can't breathe.

GRACE: *(Angry)* So leave, damn it. I don't need to be your punching bag anymore. Like it's so easy being your mother. Walking on eggshells. You're a P M S poster child. You don't know the meaning of the word "difficult." Try living with *my* mother. Now *there's* a challenge. Always telling me I'd be *nothing*. *(Takes a deep breath. Calms down)* You live a life believing you'll change things. But you don't. You wake up one morning tired, depleted, knowing you've settled. But your child—this miraculous piece of clay—maybe you can mold that into what could have been. I saw you scaling the walls of possibility. I had to push you harder. You think I liked your resenting me? *(Remembering)* That I didn't ache for the days when we held each other because we loved each other so much? When I rocked you and sang "Summertime." *(Proudly)* Oh, and you took to the sky, didn't you? You think I didn't know there was a price? All those years you barely saw me. Working hard just to avoid me. I had to get Alzheimer's to get your attention, Katie.

KATE: That is so unfair. And call me Kate, not Katie. I'm not a child.

GRACE: Certainly, as soon as you can say, "I love you."

KATE: I always tell you I love you.

GRACE: No, you say, "You *know* I love you." Big difference.

KATE: Would I be here if I didn't love you? Let's just hope I have a job left when we get back on Tuesday.

GRACE: When *you* get back on Tuesday. I'm not going.

KATE: Excuse me?

GRACE: I didn't get to see Morton Seligman.

KATE: Is it my fault he's in Europe?

GRACE: No. But he'll be back by the end of the month. We can see him after we go to your father's wedding.

KATE: We? I don't even know if *I'm* going.

GRACE: *(Coldly)* Really? I thought you were Maid of Honor.

KATE: What's that supposed to mean?

GRACE: Man meets bimbo, Man introduces daughter to bimbo, Man divorces wife for bimbo.

KATE: I never thought he would divorce you.

ACT TWO

GRACE: Forget it. That's not the issue. I simply have decided to keep traveling.

KATE: Mother, you made me a promise.

GRACE: So sue me. I'll get Johnny Cochran. He'll play the "mean daughter" card. That is if you really would let me travel alone. I was hoping you'd come with me.

KATE: And what would you use instead of Prolox? Alka Seltzer?

GRACE: I thought you could ask Sam....

KATE: *(Getting angry)* Sam? SAM? You mean the man I'm not seeing anymore because you had to leave? That Sam?

GRACE: Oh, I guess I ruined another relationship you were about to grind into the ground. So that's what this is about?

KATE: No! Yes. *(Frustrated)* OOOOH!! Every time I think you can't get any more manipulative, you trump yourself. Listen to me, Mother. I am not—underline NOT—going anywhere but back to New Jersey. And neither are you.

GRACE: Well, I guess maybe you're not so perfect after all.

KATE: *(Bursting)* No, I'm not perfect! I'm not striving to be perfect! Breaking even would be nice. *(Controlled anger)* You are an emotional sumo wrestler. And you've got to let go. I'm suffocating from you. *(Uncontrollable—furiously fast—almost without a breath)* You want to know why you're not in my life? Because every time I let you in, you want to take over the whole show. Whenever I call, you tell me what to do—what I've done wrong—why I'm *perfect*—except in the following seventy-two categories. You want to know why I'm not married? Because *you* don't want me to repeat your marrying

Mister "Oh-God-did-I-make-a-mistake-and-screw-up-my-life." So no one is ever good enough for need-a-touchup, sallow-complexioned, slovenly dressed "perfect" me. I'm goddamned petrified of relationships. Sex I can handle—fast, impersonal—that's my specialty. But *real*?—no one can stamp out a relationship faster than I—I should have a fucking page in Guinness. So I become the writer you didn't have time to be—which is a crock, because anyone can make time if she wants—but, okay, so I act out your dream. And much to my amazement I'm good at it, I own it, I fucking *love* it. And now you expect me to cancel my career and ride off into the sunset with you? Well, that's not going to happen. I am hereby reclaiming my life. It is mine. And you'll have no Prolox and I will not allow you to regress on my watch. We are going back to the nursing home—as agreed upon—and IF IT TAKES A STRAIGHT JACKET TO GET YOU THERE, *LADY*, THEN THAT'S EXACTLY HOW IT'S GOING TO WORK. *END OF DISCUSSION*!

GRACE: *(Loathingly)* I will never forgive you for being so hateful. Did I ever tell you I don't even like you?

KATE: Yes. Just not in those specific words.

(GRACE *exits.* KATE *sits down at her computer, looking pained.*)

KATE: Shit!

(KATE *walks back to the nursing home.* SAM *is going over test results.*)

SAM: According to these tests, there's no discernible change. She's fine.

KATE: Except that she won't talk to me. Which seems to be the general theme around here.

SAM: Her labs will be back this afternoon. I'll know more then.

ACT TWO

KATE: I must be looking pretty sexy to you again now that my mother's back on experiment row and I can give you a hard time again, huh?

SAM: I'll pass. You want to fight, fight with yourself.

KATE: No, no you're not leaving until we have this out. I've gotten enough rejection slips this week. Everybody seems to have a laundry list of how I disappointed them so go ahead—take your best shot.

SAM: We had a relationship, Kate. Maybe not to you because we didn't have sex so it may not qualify.

KATE: Do you know how many double lattes and pastries I had with you? I gained almost five pounds. To a woman that's a relationship.

SAM: To me, too.

KATE: I shared more of who I am with you than I did with the guy whose name I can't remember right now, but almost married....

SAM: Brad Sanger. You were a cad to Brad.

KATE: You were really listening.

SAM: I listened to everything you said. That's why I fell in love with you, damn it. It didn't compute that if you cared about me you would put my project in that kind of jeopardy.

KATE: You mean as opposed to my mother?

SAM: Of course your mother, but...

KATE: The greater good, right?

SAM: It's a war, Kate.

KATE: Yes and you're the general. But it's the privates who get killed.

SAM: Why are you making this so difficult?

KATE: Hey, you want easy, call Lorna.

SAM: Do you think I *like* you giving me a hard time?

KATE: I don't think anyone stays with me who doesn't. And I'm exhausted from it. I always have to be on for everybody.

SAM: Not with me, you don't.

KATE: Really? Look, I respect your integrity, I brought my mother back, didn't I? Can we go back to that sentence you said?

SAM: You were a cad to Brad?

KATE: "That's why I fell in love with you, damn it?"

SAM: I did love you. I do love you.

KATE: Look, Sam, you walked away from this commitment as easily as I did. It just looks better on you because you're a gentleman and I'm a street fighter.

SAM: It doesn't *feel* better.

KATE: Then fight for me, damn it, like you fought for my mother. You've obviously got it bad for the Griswald women.

(SAM *smiles. He walks to her and they kiss like a hot couple ready to do the nasty.*)

(KATE *walks to her office, doing a little dance as she goes. She begins perusing a script.* MADGE *enters, carrying two glasses of champagne.*)

MADGE: Aren't you going to join the celebration?

KATE: I'll pass.

MADGE: How often does a Saturday night show break into the top ten? Try something new—enjoy yourself.

KATE: I'm going to see my mother.

MADGE: You're the only person I know who would celebrate this in a nursing home. *(Realizing)* Sorry. How is she?

KATE: Well, she's back in the clinical trial. She seems fine. She's not talking to me. Business as usual.

MADGE: And your dad?

KATE: Warren Beatty? He's getting married this weekend.

MADGE: Really? What are you wearing?

KATE: A Vera Wang shroud. *(Beat)* I'm not going. What he did wasn't right. Going would condone it.

MADGE: It must be wonderful to have no grays in your life.

KATE: Oh, Madge, I'm conflicted about everything. It just comes out black or white. It's a technique I learned in survival school.

MADGE: Kate, when I was fourteen, I found my father in bed with our maid—which, I suppose, explained why our house was so filthy. Well, of course, I didn't tell my mother. That just wasn't done. But neither would I speak to my father again, no matter how much he begged. He had to pay, after all, for his transgression and I elected myself his jury. On my seventeenth birthday, I decided I would forgive him. *(Beat)* By providence, that was the same day he was killed protecting a total stranger from a mugger. My father was, after all, a basically decent man. *(Shakes her head sadly)* Life, I have discovered, rarely hands you a second chance. Go to the wedding. If not for him, for you.

KATE: Thank you, Madge.

MADGE: So, now that we've crawled back into the top ten, will you be less demanding?

KATE: *More.* How about you?

MADGE: Impossible!

KATE: Why fight a winning formula?

(They lift glasses and toast each other.)

MADGE/KATE: Bitch. *(Clink glasses and smile)*

(JACK and LORNA's house. JACK is dressed as Romeo, LORNA as Cleopatra in a wedding gown.)

LORNA: Come on honey, let's rehearse one last time.

(JACK and LORNA joyously belt out and dance to You're Getting To Be A Habit with Me.)

JACK: *(Singing)* Every kiss, every hug
Seems to act just like a drug
You're getting to be a habit with me.

LORNA: *(Singing)* Let me stay in your arms
I'm addicted to your charms
You're getting to be a habit with me.

(KATE enters.)

JACK: Katie! I'm so glad you came.

KATE: Me too, Daddy.

LORNA: Watch. It's for the reception. This represents us.

(KATE watches this with humor and disbelief. During this GRACE enters, unseen, and watches the twosome. She has dyed her hair blond and looks very glamorous.)

JACK/LORNA: *(Singing)* But now I couldn't do without my supply
I need you for my own.
Oh I can't get away
I must have you every day
As regularly as coffee or tea.

ACT TWO

You've got me in your clutches and I can't get free
You're getting to be a habit with me.
Can't break it.
You're getting to be a habit with me.
Can't shake it.
You're getting to be a habit with me.

(KATE *applauds.*)

RABBI: (*Offstage*) Can I see the bride and groom, please.

LORNA: We're coming Rabbi...hold your tallis.

(LORNA *and* JACK *exit.*)

GRACE: Now that's entertainment.

KATE: (*Spins to see her*) You came.

GRACE: I never miss any of your father's weddings.

KATE: Mom...

(GRACE *puts up a hand to silence her.*)

GRACE: Don't worry, I'm on twenty-four-hours shore leave. I have my medication.

KATE: Where did you get?

GRACE: Did you know they don't always lock the medicine cabinets? Very careless.

KATE: Oh my God, grand larceny now?

GRACE: Katie, of all people you should know, what Grace wants, Grace gets. I'm going home tomorrow.

KATE: Look at your hair. You're a babe.

GRACE: If I only have one life, let me live it as a blond.

KATE: So you're talking to me again?

GRACE: As long as you don't blow my cover.
I'm appealing to you as a mother who went through twenty-three excruciating hours of childbirth without an epidural.

KATE: Mom, all they want is a nice quiet wedding.

GRACE: Don't worry. I just thought I'd give the happy couple a surprise. *(Beat)* Think Pearl Harbor.

(JACK *enters.*)

JACK: I want to...

(Sees GRACE, *amazed)*

JACK: Grace? Is that really you? Kate told me about that drug...I had no idea.... You look wonderful...Alzheimer's agrees with you.

GRACE: I would have preferred a spa.

JACK: Your hair—I like it blond.

GRACE: Speaking of hair, I think something landed on your head.

JACK: It's a wig.

GRACE: No...

JACK: Lorna says it makes me look younger.

LORNA: *(Reentering)* Jackie, I need you in the kitchen.... *(Stops)*

JACK: Look who's here, Lorna, it's Grace.

GRACE: You remember—the glassy-eyed woman from the wheelchair?

LORNA: *(Sincerely)* Oh, my gosh, Grace, I'm so happy to meet you.

GRACE: *(Thrown)* Jack, I think you've met your match.

LORNA: It's weird cause usually Geminis don't get along this well. But us, we're two peas in a pod, aren't we, Punkin?

GRACE: Punkin? *(Picks up a vase)* This is proof positive people marry the same people all over again. *(To* LORNA*)* You won't believe how similar our taste is. This

Italian vase, that Chagall lithograph, even the Queen Anne chair over there. Dead ringers for things we had in our home in New Jersey.

JACK: They *are* from our house in Jersey.

LORNA: The bean bag chairs and the lava lamp are from my first marriage. We left a ton in the house in Jersey.

GRACE: That was very considerate.

LORNA: You see, we sort of didn't think you were coming back.

GRACE: Surprise!

LORNA: I want you to know, Grace, that I absolutely adore Jackie. I'm going to do everything I can to make him happy.

GRACE: Well, that's a load off my mind.

(*Silence as everyone shifts uncomfortably in his chair.*)

LORNA: Can we offer you something to drink, Grace?

GRACE: How about a pina colada. Or are you two just using that in the shower?

JACK: What?

LORNA: (*To* JACK) You told Grace about that?

JACK: Of course not.

GRACE: Listen, I don't want you two kids fighting on your nuptial day. Jack didn't tell me. I heard it when he told Katie about the pussycat feather duster you use.

LORNA: You told your daughter about the pussycats?

(JACK *tries, but can't speak.*)

GRACE: Punkin, your fiancée asked you a question.

LORNA: I mean, that's even sicker than telling your ex-wife.

GRACE: It is pretty perverse, isn't it?

LORNA: There are some things that are private, Jack Griswald. Like the showers I'm going to be taking from now on. *(Storms out of the room.)*

GRACE: I'd like to speak to your father alone.

(JACK *faces* KATE *and motions for her not to leave.* KATE *exits.*)

GRACE: Quite a temper on that Lorna. Bad for her jowls. Definitely a candidate for Botox. By the way, your rug is gliding to the right.

JACK: She'll never speak to me again.

GRACE: At fifty-two it's not so easy to find someone. I'm telling you, there must be a tote board in Miami... *(As though reading sign)* Single man with pulse enters State. *(Imitating* JACK*)* Ka-ching, ka-ching.

JACK: *(Looks amazed at* GRACE*)* You heard me? Everything I said?

GRACE: Not always. Some. Enough.

JACK: Well, you look terrific. You always had the best pair of legs in the business. Better than Grable's. And now, with this new look—you look exactly like the girl I fell in love with.

GRACE: Which one? *(Beat)* There should be one of those Surgeon General warnings on marriage licenses. I'm not saying it was all your fault. I'll take my twenty percent.

JACK: I always end up disappointing you, don't I?

GRACE: You were fun, I had great legs, it should have been two dates—not marriage. *(Beat)* Well, Lorna's silicon duo is very perky. I assume she gives fellatio?

JACK: Grace!

ACT TWO

GRACE: *(Turning the knife)* Just cause I didn't do doesn't mean I didn't know.

JACK: What should I do, Grace?

GRACE: Jack, you owed it to me to stay. You don't bury someone before she's dead. For better or for worse, that's what it's supposed to be.

JACK: Do you want me to leave Lorna?

GRACE: Yes. Go get packed. The cab is waiting. We're leaving in ten minutes.

JACK: *(Panicked)* I...I...

GRACE: Oh, for God's sake, Jack, I don't want you to leave Lorna. I'd like you to want to. To yearn for me so passionately, you'd be willing to leave her and never look back. But I wouldn't actually want you to do it.

JACK: Gracie, I always felt more than I showed.

GRACE: I know.

JACK: I am profoundly sorry for being a jerk.

GRACE: Thank you.

(KATE *breathes this moment in.*)

GRACE: Well, I think I'll be going now.

JACK: Why?

GRACE: *(Deadpan)* Because I'm crushed you didn't ask me to be a bridesmaid. Jack, I have a plane to catch. *(Smiles)* Lorna seems very nice. So, I wish you a happy life. Go be with her.

(JACK *tries to kiss* GRACE *goodbye, but she pulls away.* JACK *exits.*)

GRACE: You can come out now.

(KATE *comes out of shadows.*)

GRACE: Just like when you used to watch "The Brady Bunch" through the banister. You heard what we said?

KATE: Yes. That was amazingly gracious of you.

GRACE: I did what a lady does. Now you do the same. You only have one father.

KATE: Where are you going?

GRACE: A woman is entitled to a little mystery.

(GRACE *exits.* KATE *looks proudly after her mother.* JACK *enters.*)

JACK: Honey. Is anything wrong?

KATE: *(Is he kidding)* Nah.

JACK: You're still angry with me? *(Off her shrug)* I don't blame you. But the truth is your mother and I probably shouldn't have gotten married in the first place.

KATE: These are words a child appreciates hearing. *(Looks at him)* God, Daddy, why did you marry Mom?

JACK: *(Remembering)* Because I couldn't have her. She was a lady. No sex. What I didn't know was that was a sign of the next forty-two years. You know the only time I saw your mother sexy was with another man. This one night we were at a club with some friends and the band plays that tune from *Picnic*— you know, *(Singing, gets into it)* "It had to be Moonglow..." And this man I've never seen asks her to dance. Turns out it was that professor of hers, Morton Seligman. So they're on the dance floor dancing, but it's like there's no one else out there and they're making this sensual, electric love. Me, I never saw that from her. But for that moment I thought... Grace has got it in her.

LORNA: *(Singing, offstage)* Let me stay in your arms I'm addicted to your charms...

ACT TWO 71

JACK: *(Beaming)* This is what a man needs to feel. Loved. I'm sorry I failed with your mother, sweetheart.

(KATE *looks at Jack for the first time as just a human being with frailties.*)

KATE: I hope you get it right this time, Daddy.

JACK: I'm gonna go check out the chopped liver swan. *(Exits)*

KATE: Hey Lorna, you ever hear the one about Celine Dion?

LORNA: No.

KATE: You will.

(JACK *and* LORNA *exit.*)

(Moonglow, *the music from* Picnic *plays.* GRACE *and* MORTON SELIGMAN *dance in silhouette.* KATE *watches them dip and turn romantically, slowly across the stage.* GRACE *exits the stage, still floating on air. A pool of light on* GRACE *on the telephone.* KATE's *phone rings.*)

KATE: *(Sleepy)* Hello.

(*Off* GRACE's *humming*)

KATE: Mom, is that you?

GRACE: No, it's Ginger Rogers.

KATE: Mom, it's four A M.

GRACE: Oh, no. Did I break curfew? *(Beat)* I was with the great Morton Seligman. It was the most wonderful night of my life.

KATE: And morning. What were you doing all night? *(Quickly)* That was rhetorical.

GRACE: Katie, I told Morton about my journals and he says he knows a lot of important people in Washington and...he wants me to testify to Congress about Alzheimer's. What do you think? Is it ridiculous?

KATE: Absolutely not. Great idea. Girl from Ghetto galvanizes government. I like it.

GRACE: Morton also asked me to stay here with him.

KATE: *(With trepidation)* And you accepted?

GRACE: It turns out that he's in between marriages—his fourth and his fifth. He's engaged and he still asked me to stay. Can you imagine? I told him I never play the other woman.

KATE: Sam wants you back in the clinical trial.

GRACE: I'm giving it serious consideration. The shore leave may have to be extended for another twenty-four hours.

KATE: You are going to kill me.

GRACE: *(Smiling)* Do you know how manipulative that sounds?

KATE: Well, I learned at the knees of The Master. *(Beat)* Mom, about the argument we had...

GRACE: Well, that's just another thing mothers and daughters do—go for the jugular.

(KATE *hangs up the phone. She rushes into a restaurant where* SAM *is already seated with a bottle of wine. They kiss, clearly in a relationship.*)

KATE: Sorry I'm late, honey. What a crazy day. As if Madge weren't enough high maintenance for one show. Now Bootsie the Beagle refused to come out of *her* trailer.

SAM: How about some wine? *(Pours)*

KATE: Well if you insist. Did you see what my mother gave me? Her favorite pearls.

ACT TWO

SAM: Very elegant. So she didn't give them to your sister, Gwen, huh?

KATE: *(Realizing)* No. I'm the favorite. Yes! *(Beat)* So, what shall we toast?

SAM: How about "to future medical possibilities."

KATE: Whoa! There's a romantic toast.

SAM: I want to switch Grace to Kentinol.

KATE: *(Stiffens)* But the Prolox is working.

SAM: Not like it was.

KATE: It's been working for four months.

SAM: I know. I'd really like to try the Kentinol. If not, there are others. We find something new every day in biological research. You have to believe that.

KATE: *(Beat)* She's going to die, right?

SAM: I didn't say that.

KATE: But you're thinking it. I can see you thinking it.

SAM: No, actually you can't do that.

KATE: She's going to testify in front of Congress in two weeks. You know how much we've been working on her speech. For the first time we're on the same team. This is her shot. *(Beat)* Our shot. *(Beat)* Sam, will she still be able to testify?

SAM: I think so. I hope so.

KATE: It's because I took her away. Do you think I'm a bad person?

SAM: No, I think you're beautiful. *(Kisses her)* Kentinol is a very promising drug.

KATE: *(An edge)* Well then we definitely must have it. Put her on the Kentinol. *(Stares blankly as she drinks)* Did I mention what a great day it was today?

(KATE, GRACE, MADGE, MARTY *and* SAM *are in a screening room watching movie in dark.*)

SENATOR: *(V/O)* Please continue, Mrs Griswald.

MADGE: *(V/O)* This disease robs you of your soul, your dignity and ultimately your life. We can either invest today or be bankrupt tomorrow. You may think I'm selfish to request so much, but I can live with that. If you allot the needed funds for research, so can you.

(*Lights up. They applaud.* MADGE *goes to* GRACE.)

MADGE: When Kate showed me the tape of you testifying in the Senate, I knew I had to play you in the movie. Did I do you proud?

(GRACE *speaks less assuredly now.*)

GRACE: I was...pretty hot stuff out there.

MADGE: You were a showstopper. (*To* KATE) I think I'll go home and dust off the mantle for my next Emmy.

(MADGE *and* KATE *hug.* MADGE *exits.*)

GRACE: Today my words were heard in the Senate of the United States of America.

KATE: No. That was six months ago in front of six senators and seventy-five people. But this H B O movie will reach twenty million homes.

GRACE: Twenty million. Can you imagine? Me, Grace Hirshfeld...

KATE: Griswald.

GRACE: A lady who never lived up to her potential....

KATE: Well you delivered.

GRACE: None of this could have happened without you.... Know that and... (*Points to* KATE's *heart*) ...keep it with you there.

ACT TWO

(KATE, *unable to speak, shakes her head yes.*)

GRACE: I love you unreservedly, *Kate*...because you're my daughter, and that's what mothers do.

(They hug long and hard.)

GRACE: Okay, let's not get maudlin.

KATE *leads* GRACE *back to where the nursing home has been. Although now struggling with her balance,* GRACE *remains strong verbally. While speaking,* KATE *helps* GRACE *change into her robe.)*

GRACE: I have some things to tell you. First of all, it's time for you to get on with your life. I also can suggest with whom.

KATE: I'll bet.

GRACE: He's a very nice boy.

KATE: Yes.

GRACE: Also, I want to stay a blond. I detest strained peas. I don't wear itchy wool sweaters. Only cashmere. Imported.

KATE: I would expect nothing less. *(Looks at her mother)* I hate Alzheimer's.

GRACE: I have it. That's how the chips fell. It's no one's fault.

KATE: I have to be able to direct this anger at someone.

GRACE: *(Now in her robe, smiles)* So be like everyone else. Blame the Jews.

(KATE *is on the phone with* JACK *and* LORNA.)

KATE: Well, good news, it's only a minor hip fracture.

LORNA: Thank God.

JACK: Do you want us to come up and be with you?

KATE: No, I'm okay.

LORNA: Because if you need us we're there in three hours.

KATE: Thanks, Lorna.

JACK: Hey, we're family. Just a little extended.

(Pool of light on MADGE *on the phone with* KATE*)*

MADGE: But she seemed so disoriented when I went to see her.

KATE: It's the pain medicine. Once they ease off the high dosage, she should be more coherent.

MADGE: Oh, sweetie, she's so in and out...one minute she's talking to me...?

KATE: I know. Time to buckle up and go back on the roller coaster again. That's the way this disease works.

MADGE: You know, ever since I did the movie, you can't believe how many people I talk to about Alzheimer's, their mothers, their husbands.

KATE: I know.

MADGE: Do they have a telethon for this? I could do a couple of numbers from *Gypsy (Sings out)* "Small world, isn't it...funny...."

KATE: Thank you, Madge.

(Smiles. She walks to GRACE's *room at the hospital.)*

KATE: Hi Mom. It's Kate. Look, I brought you a pillow.

(Off GRACE's *smile)*

KATE: It says "Mirror, mirror on the wall. I am my mother after all."

GRACE: *(Haltingly)* That's beautiful.

KATE: *(Meaning it)* I agree.

GRACE: Unless we're talking about my mother. Then it's vicious.

ACT TWO

(KATE *and* GRACE *laugh.*)

GRACE: *(Realizing)* Did you hear me? That was mama's laugh. I like that. Part of... *(Searching for a phrase)*

KATE: *(Finishing)* ...life's cycle.

GRACE: *(Rambling, upset)* I want to go to college.

KATE: What, Mom?

GRACE: *(Getting upset, she looks right at* KATE*)*
It's not fair, Mama. I'm smarter than he is.

KATE: *(Trying to comfort her)* I know, I know...you are smarter.

GRACE: Tell Papa.

KATE: I will. I will. You're okay, Mom. You're safe.

GRACE: Nothing was ever enough for her. I did that to you.

KATE: It doesn't matter anymore. *(Trying to divert her)* Look at those roses. That's the third bouquet you've gotten from the great Morton Seligman. You know, you're having a better social life than half my single friends.

(KATE *gets up and walks to the audience.*)

KATE: If I had known how little time we had left before it began, I would have devoted every waking moment to being with my mother.

(It is months later. SAM *is going over the charts with her.)*

SAM: We cleared up the pneumonia, but it's not the Alzheimer's that kills a patient; it's the complications. I'm afraid the old fighter in Grace isn't kicking in.

(KATE *walks to* GRACE *who is in the wheelchair, visibly more fragile.* GRACE *is off in her own world.*)

KATE: You may never give up. I did not come all this way only to find out my mother is a quitter. We are going to take every medication offered until Sam finds a way to help you. Okay? *(Getting her attention)* Okay?

GRACE: *(Forming an "O")* Oh...kay.

SAM: She hears you, all right.

KATE: Of course she does.

SAM: Then hear this, Grace. Your hip is all healed now. Be careful with it. I want you to be able to dance at Kate's and my wedding.

KATE: You certainly don't think that feeble pronouncement is going to pass as a proposal, do you?

SAM: Don't worry, I know with whom I'm dealing. I'm flying down to Miami to ask for your hand officially. Then we can choose a ring.

KATE: Forget that. Just go discover a cure.

SAM: That's what I love. You are the only woman I know who would send me to a lab over Tiffany's.

KATE: Who said anything about not going to Tiffany's?

(They kiss. SAM exits. KATE walks over to GRACE.)

KATE: Well, it looks like the very nice boy and I may have a future together after all. That happened because of you, you know. Well, of course you know. I love you, Mom.

GRACE: *(Her eyes suddenly clear)* How can you love me?

KATE: Because you're my mommy. The best in the world. *(Tears roll down her face)* So hang in there. Will you do that for me? Hang in there.

(Beat, trying to get GRACE's rapt attention)

KATE: So maybe I should have a granddaughter for you. You'd like that wouldn't you? With *the doctor* you wanted me to marry. As though I stood a chance. What Grace wants, Grace gets. *(Beat)* I bet she'll be just like you, Mom. All that love and determination in one little package. Boy, am *I* in trouble.

*(*KATE *looks at* GRACE *and laughs.* GRACE, *seeing* KATE *laughing, joins in.)*

END OF PLAY

www.ingramcontent.com/pod-product-compliance
Lightning Source LLC
Chambersburg PA
CBHW060213050426
42446CB00013B/3062